This Book
Belongs To:

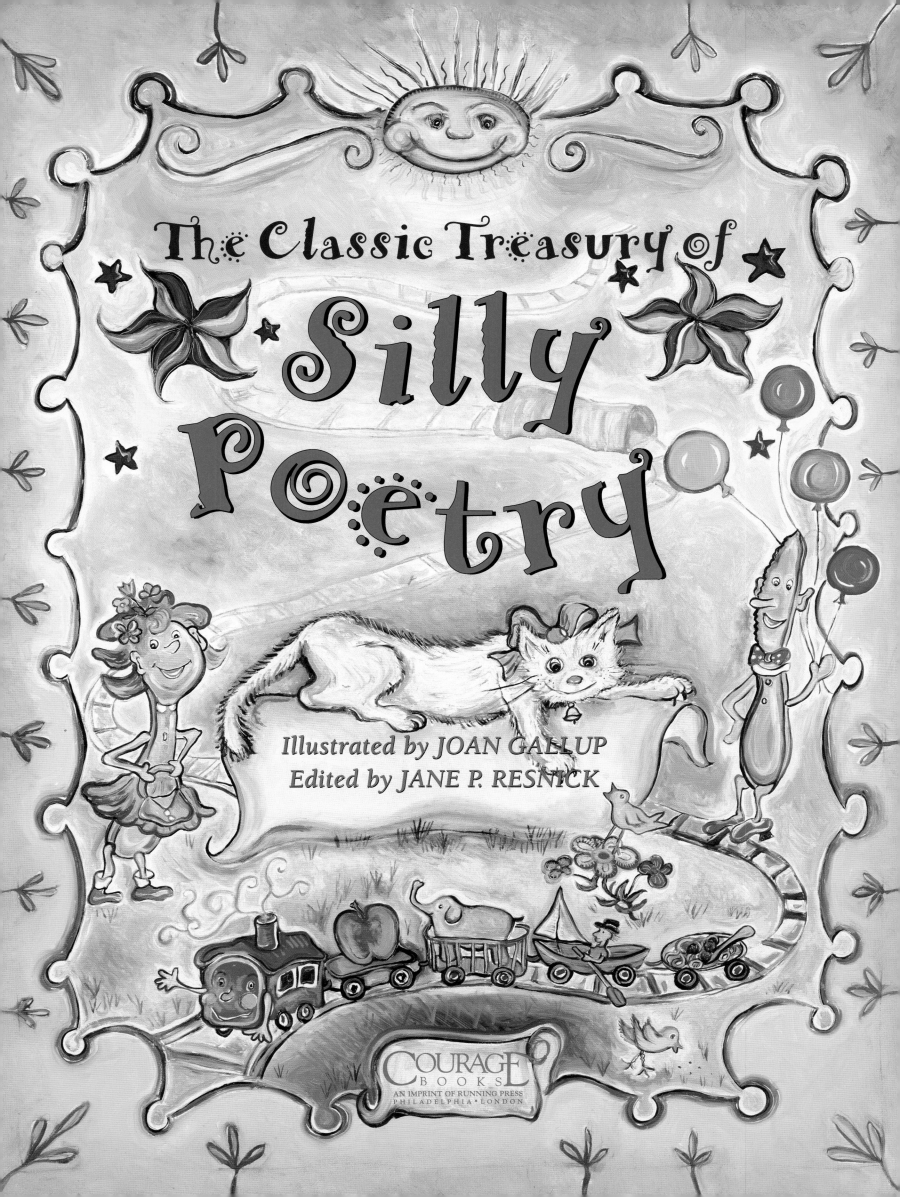

The Classic Treasury of

Silly Poetry

Illustrated by JOAN GALLUP
Edited by JANE P. RESNICK

COURAGE
BOOKS
AN IMPRINT OF RUNNING PRESS
PHILADELPHIA • LONDON

9 8 7
Digit on the right indicates the number of this printing.

Library of Congress Cataloging-in-Publication Number 94–73894

ISBN 1–56138–486–0

Cover and interior designs by Christian T. Benton
Cover and interior illustrations by Joan Gallup

Permissions credits: "Clock" from *Small Poems* by Valerie Worth.
                         Copyright © 1972 by Valerie Worth.
                         Reprinted by permission of Farrar, Straus, & Giroux, Inc.

                         "Eletelephony" from *Tirra Lirra: Rhymes Old and New*
                         by Laura Richards. Copyright © 1930, 1932 by Laura Richards.
                         Copyright © renewed 1960 by Hamilton Richards.
                         Reprinted by permission of Little, Brown and Company.

                         "Jellyfish Stew" from *The New Kid on the Block*
                         by Jack Prelutsky. Copyright © 1984 by Jack Prelutsky.
                         Reprinted by permission of Greenwillow Books, a division of
                         William Morrow & Company, Inc.

Published by Courage Books, an imprint of
Running Press Book Publishers
125 South Twenty-second Street
Philadelphia, Pennsylvania 19103–4399

introduction

There's a surprise waiting in this treasury of poems.

The poems have rhythm, of course—read them, and listen for the music of the words. They have rhyme, too—say the words aloud and make them sing. Some of these poems tell the truth. Others make up stories. Some are sweet, and some are strange. But most of all, these poems are full of giggles, chuckles, and great big laughs! They're surprisingly, delightfully, splendidly funny!

Peanuts and peas, umbrellas and hummingbirds, porcupines and flimflams: these are the subjects that poems are made of! Imagine classic writers and respected poets, from Rudyard Kipling to Edward Lear, writing about pobbles who have no toes, about elephants who try to use telephones, and about camels who chant!

Silly? Yes! Ridiculous? Absolutely! But that's why it's so fun! When words twist and sounds turn, the result is an incredible blossom of blustery poetry.

So read on, and *laugh till it hurts*.

Contents

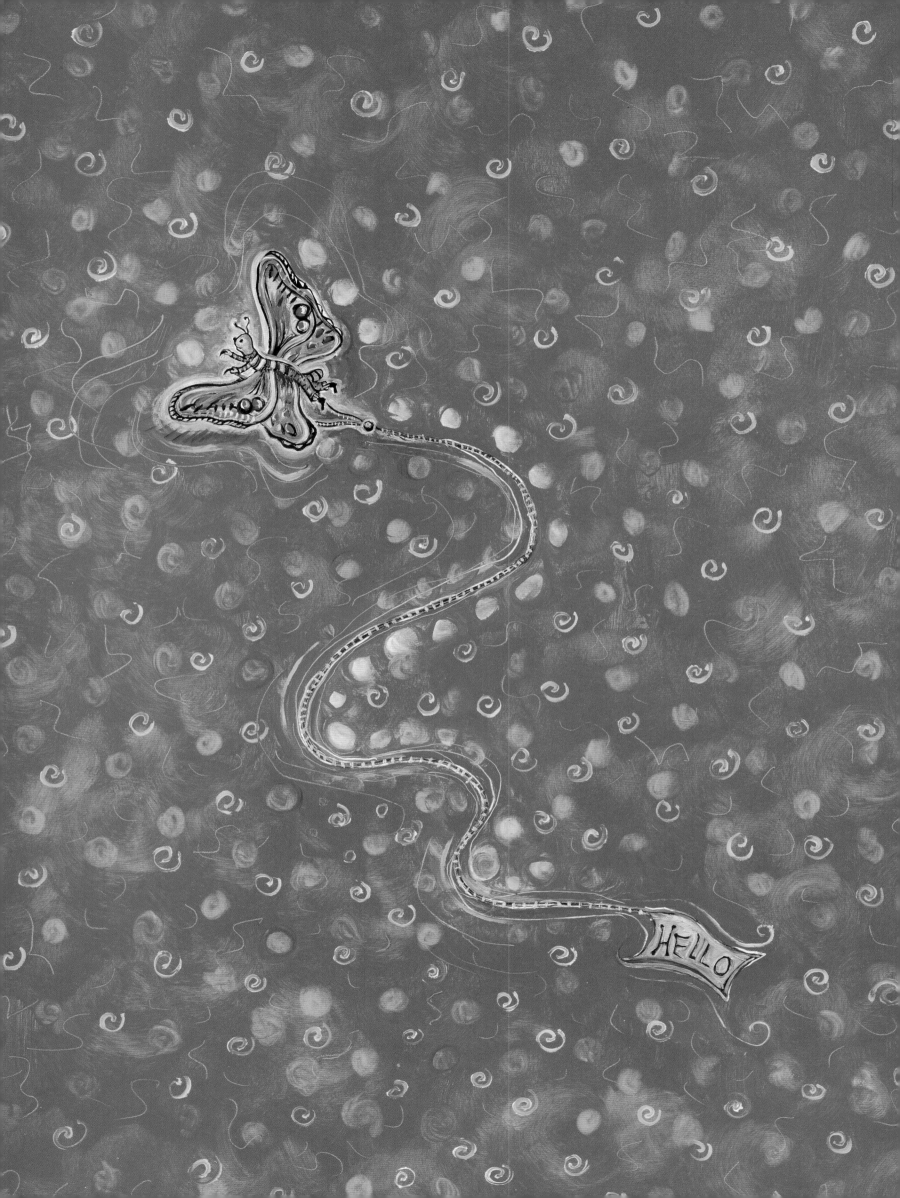

Jellyfish Stew

Jellyfish Stew
I'm longing for you
I dearly adore you
oh, truly, I do,
you're creepy to see,
revolting to chew
you slide down inside with a hullaballo.

You're soggy, you're smelly
you taste like shampoo
you bog down my belly
with oodles of goo,
yet I would glue noodles
and prunes to my shoe
for one oozy spoonful
of Jellyfish Stew.

—*Jack Prelutsky*

Clock

This clock
Has stopped,
Some gear
Or spring
Gone wrong—
Too tight,
Or cracked,
Or choked
With dust;
A year
Has passed
Since last
It said
Ting ting
Or tick
Or tock.
Poor
Clock.

—*Valerie Worth*

Eletelephony

Once there was an elephant,
Who tried to use the telephant—
No! No! I mean an elephone
Who tried to use the telephone—
(Dear me! I am not certain quite
That even now I've got it right.)

Howe'er it was, he got his trunk
Entangled in the telephunk;
The more he tried to get it free,
The louder buzzed the telephee—

—*Laura E. Richards*

Hey, Diddle, Diddle!

Hey, diddle, diddle!
The cat and the fiddle,
The cow jumped over the moon;
The little dog laughed
To see such sport,
And the dish ran away
with the spoon.

—Mother Goose

The Cow Slips Away

The tall pines pine,
The pawpaws pause,
    And the bumblebee bumbles all day;

The eavesdropper drops,
And the grasshopper hops,
    While gently the cow slips away.

—Ben King

13

A Sleeper

A sleeper from the Amazon
Put nighties of his gra'mazon—
The reason, that
He was too fat
To get his own pajamazon.

—*Anonymous*

A Nobleman Dining at Crewe

A nobleman, dining at Crewe,
Found quite a large mouse in his stew.
Said the waiter, "Don't shout,
And wave it about,
Or the rest will be wanting one, too!"

—Anonymous

Stately Verse

If Mary goes far out to sea
        By wayward breezes fanned,
I'd like to know—can you tell me?—
        Just where would Maryland?

If Tenny went high up in air
        And looked o'er land and sea,
Looked here and there and everywhere,
        Pray what would Tennessee?

I looked out of the window and
        Saw Orry on the lawn;
He's not there now, and who can tell
        Just where has Oregon?

Two girls were quarreling one day
        With garden tools, and so
I said, "My dears, let Mary rake
        And just let Idaho."

A friend o' mine lived in a flat
        With half a dozen boys;
When he fell ill I asked him why.
        He said: "I'm Illinois."

An English lady had a steed.
        She called him "Ighland Bay."
She rode for exercise, and thus
        Rhode Island every day.

—*Anonymous*

Estella's Umbrella

There was a wee girl named Estella
Who owned an enormous umbrella;
    Till one day in a gale
    With lightning and hail
The umbrella went up with Estella.

–Mabel B. Hill

From "The September Gale"

It chanced to be our washing day,
    And all our things were drying;
The storm came roaring through the lines,
    And set them all a-flying;
I saw the shirts and petticoats
    Go riding off like witches;
I lost, ah! bitterly I wept,—
    I lost my Sunday breeches!

I saw them straddling through the air,
    Alas! too late to win them;
I saw them chase the clouds, as if
    The devil had been in them;
They were my darlings and my pride,
    My boyhood's only riches,—
"Farewell, farewell," I faintly cried,—
"My breeches! O my breeches!"

—Oliver Wendell Holmes

19

The Song of the All-Wool Shirt

My father bought an undershirt
    Of bright and flaming red—
"All wool, I'm ready to assert,
    Fleece-dyed," the merchant said;
"Your size is thirty-eight, I think;
    A forty you should get,
Since all-wool goods are bound to shrink
    A trifle when they're wet."

That shirt two weeks my father wore—
    Two washings, that was all;
From forty down to thirty-four
    It shrank like a leaf in fall.
I wore it then a day or two,
    But when 'twas washed again
My wife said, "Now 'twill only do
    For little brother Ben."

A fortnight Ben squeezed into it;
    At last he said it hurt.
We put it on our babe—the fit
    Was good as any shirt.
We ne'er will wash it more while yet
    We see its flickering light,
For if again that shirt is wet
    'Twill vanish from our sight.

—*Eugene Field*

Peas

I always eat peas with honey,
I've done it all my life.
They do taste kind of funny,
But it keeps them on the knife.

—*Anonymous*

There Was a Young Lady of Niger

There was a young lady of Niger
Who smiled as she rode on a tiger;
    They returned from the ride
    With the lady inside,
And the smile on the face of the tiger.

—*Cosmo Monkhouse*

The Prayer of Cyrus Brown

"The proper way for a man to pray,"
    Said Deacon Lemuel Keyes,
"And the only proper attitude
    Is down upon his knees."

"No, I should say the way to pray,"
    Said Rev. Doctor Wise,
"Is standing straight with outstretched arms
    And rapt and upturned eyes."

"Last year I fell in Hodgkin's well
    Head first," said Cyrus Brown,
"With both my heels a stickin' up,
    My head a-pinting down;

"An' I made a prayer right then an' there—
    Best prayer I ever said,
The prayingest prayer I ever prayed,
    A-standing on my head."

—Sam Walter Foss

There Was an Old Man of Blackheath

There was an old man of Blackheath
Who sat on his set of false teeth.
    Said he, with a start,
      "O Lord, bless my heart!
I've bitten myself underneath!"

—Anonymous

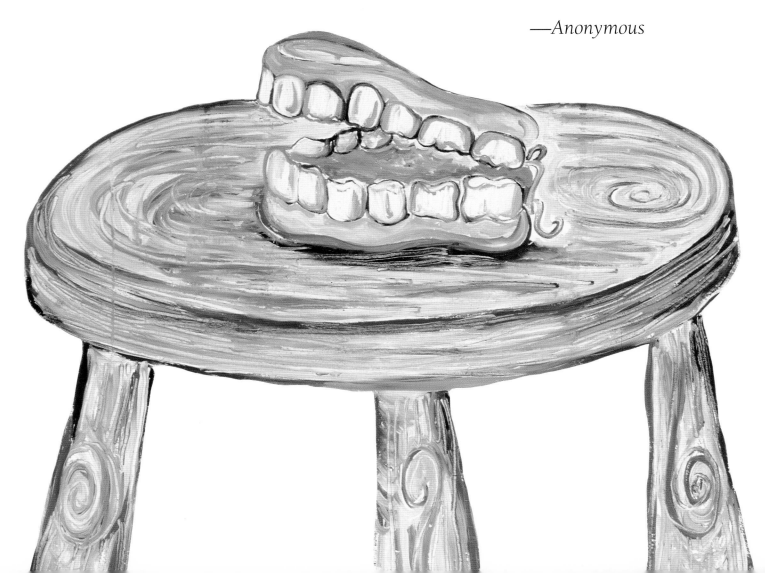

The Pobble Who Has No Toes

The Pobble who has no toes
    Had once as many as we;
When they said, "Some day you may lose them;"
    He replied, "Fish fiddle de-dee!"
And his Aunt Jobiska made him drink
Lavender water tinged with pink;
For she said, "The World in general knows
There's nothing so good for a Pobble's toes!"

The Pobble who has no toes,
    Swam across the Bristol Channel;
But before he set out he wrapped his nose
    In a piece of scarlet flannel.
For his Aunt Jobiska said, "No harm
Can come to his toes if his nose is warm;
And it's perfectly known that a Pobble's toes
Are safe—provided he minds his nose."

The Pobble swam fast and well,
    And when boats or ships came near him,
He tinkledy-blinkledy-winkled a bell
    So that all the world could hear him.
And all the Sailors and Admirals cried,
When they saw him nearing the further side,—
"He has gone to fish for his Aunt Jobiska's
Runcible Cat with crimson whiskers!"

But before he touched the shore,—
  The shore of the Bristol Channel,
A sea-green Porpoise carried away
  His wrapper of scarlet flannel.
And when he came to observe his feet,
Formerly garnished with toes so neat,
His face at once became forlorn
On perceiving that all his toes were gone!

And nobody ever knew,
    From that dark day to the present,
Whoso had taken the Pobble's toes,
    In a manner so far from pleasant.
Whether the shrimps or crawfish grey,
Or crafty Mermaids stole them away,
Nobody knew; and nobody knows
How the Pobble was robbed of his twice five toes!

The Pobble who has no toes
    Was placed in a friendly Bark,
And they rowed him back, and carried him up
    To his Aunt Jobiska's Park.
And she made him a feast, at his earnest wish,
Of eggs and buttercups fried with fish;
And she said, "It's a fact the whole world knows,
That Pobbles are happier without their toes."

—*Edward Lear*

The Twins

In form and feature, face and limb,
  I grew so like my brother,
That folks got taking me for him
  And each for one another.
It puzzled all our kith and kin,
  It reached an awful pitch;
For one of us was born a twin,
  Yet not a soul knew which.

One day (to make the matter worse),
  Before our names were fixed,
As we were being washed by nurse
  We got completely mixed;
And thus, you see, by Fate's decree,
  (Or rather nurse's whim),
My brother John got christened me,
  And I got christened *him*.

This fatal likeness even dogg'd
  My footsteps when at school,
And I was always getting flogg'd,
  For John turned out a fool.
I put this question hopelessly
  To everyone I knew—
What would you do, if you were me,
  To prove that you were *you*?

Our close resemblance turned the tide
  Of my domestic life;
For somehow my intended bride
  Became my brother's wife.
In short, year after year the same
  Absurd mistake went on;
And when I died—the neighbors came
  And buried brother John!

—*Henry S. Leigh*

There Was a Naughty Boy

There was a naughty boy
And a naughty boy was he.
He ran away to Scotland,
The people for to see.
But he found
That the ground
Was as hard,
That a yard
Was as long,
That a song
Was as merry,
That a cherry
Was as red,
That lead
Was as weighty,
That fourscore
Was still eighty,
And a door was as wooden as in England.
So he stood in his shoes and he wondered,
He wondered, he wondered,
So he stood in his shoes and he wondered.

—*John Keats*

Wilhelmina Mergenthaler

Wilhelmina Mergenthaler
Had a lovely ermine collar
Made of just the nicest fur,
That her mamma bought for her.
Once, when mamma was away
Out a-shopping for the day,
Wilhelmina Mergenthaler
Ate her lovely ermine collar.

—*Harry P. Taber*

There Once Was a Barber of Kew

There once was a barber of Kew,
Who went very mad at the Zoo;
He tried to enamel
The face of the camel,
And gave the brown bear a shampoo.

—*Cosmo Monkhouse*

Godfrey Gordon Gustavus Gore

Godfrey Gordon Gustavus Gore—
No doubt you have heard the name before—
Was a boy who never would shut a door!

The wind might whistle, the wind might roar,
And teeth be aching and throats be sore,
But still he never would shut the door.

His father would beg, his mother implore.
"Godfrey Gordon Gustavus Gore,
We really *do* wish you would shut the door!"

Their hands they wrung, their hair they tore;
But Godfrey Gordon Gustavus Gore
Was deaf as the buoy out at the Nore.

When he walked forth the folks would roar,
"Godfrey Gordon Gustavus Gore
Why don't you think to shut the door?"

They rigged out a Shutter with sail and oar,
And threatened to pack off Gustavus Gore
On a voyage of penance to Singapore.

But he begged for mercy, and said, "No more!
Pray do not send me to Singapore
On a Shutter, and then I will shut the door!"

"You will?" said his parents; "then keep on shore!
But mind you do! For the plague is sore
Of a fellow that never will shut the door,
Godfrey Gordon Gustavus Gore!"

—*William Brighty Rands*

The Ingenious Little Old Man

A little old man of the sea
Went out in a boat for a sail,
The water came in
almost up to his chin
And he had nothing with which to bail.

But this little old man of the sea
Just drew out his jacknife so stout,
And a hole with its blade
In the bottom he made,
So that all of the water ran out.

—*John Bennett*

Uncle

Uncle, whose inventive brains
Kept evolving aeroplanes,
Fell from an enormous height
On my garden lawn, last night.
    Flying is a fatal sport,
    Uncle wrecked the tennis court.

—Harry Graham

From "Science for the Young"

Arthur with a lighted taper
Touched the fire to grandpa's paper.
Grandpa leaped a foot or higher,
Dropped the sheet and shouted "Fire!"
Arthur, wrapped in contemplation,
Viewed the scene of conflagration.
"This," he said, "confirms my notion—
Heat creates both light and motion."

—Wallace Irwin

Oh, No!

Oh, no!
'Tisn't so!
Papa's watch
Won't go?

It *must* go—
Guess I know!
Last night
I wound it tight,
And greased it nice
With camphor-ice.

—*Mary Mapes Dodge*

My Face

As a beauty I'm not a great star,
There are others more handsome by far,
But my face I don't mind it,
Because I'm behind it—
'Tis the folks in the front that I jar!

—*Anthony Euwer*

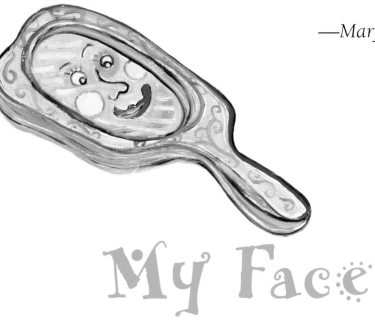

The Blind Men and the Elephant

It was six men of Indostan,
        To learning much inclined,
Who went to see the Elephant
        (Though all of them were blind),
That each by observation
        Might satisfy his mind.

The First approached the Elephant,
        And happening to fall
Against his broad and sturdy side,
        At once began to bawl:
"God bless me! but the Elephant
        Is very like a wall!"

The Second, feeling of the tusk,
    Cried, "Ho! what have we here
So very round and smooth and sharp?
    To me 'tis mighty clear
This wonder of an Elephant
    Is very like a spear!"

The Third approached the animal,
    And happening to take
The squirming trunk within his hands,
    Thus boldly up and spake:
"I see," quoth he, "the Elephant
    Is very like a snake!"

The Fourth reached out his eager hand,
    And felt about the knee.
"What most this wondrous beast is like
    Is mighty plain," quoth he;
"'Tis clear enough the Elephant
    Is very like a tree!"

The Fifth, who chanced to touch the ear,
     Said: "E'en the blindest man
Can tell what this resembles most;
     Deny the fact who can,
This marvel of an Elephant
     Is very like a fan!"

The Sixth no sooner had begun
     About the beast to grope,
Than, seizing on the swinging tail
     That fell within his scope,
"I see," quoth he, "the Elephant
     Is very like a rope!"

And so these men of Indostan
     Disputed loud and long,
Each in his own opinion
     Exceeding stiff and strong,
Though each was partly in the right,
     And all were in the wrong!

—*John Godfrey Saxe*

From "Story of Reginald"

Cousin Reg is a charming boy—
Just like little Lord Fauntleroy.
All day long he sweetly prattles
O' animals, fairies, kings, and battles.

Dear little chap . . . he bores me stiff!
We'll go for a walk to the top of the cliff;
The cliff is steep and it's lonely, too—
What an adventure, Reg, for you.

Cousin Reg was a charming boy,
Just like little Lord Fauntleroy. . . .

—*Hubert Phillips*

The Ichthyosaurus

There once was an Ichthyosaurus,
Who lived when the earth was all porous,
But he fainted with shame
When he first heard his name,
And departed a long time before us.

—*Isabel Frances Bellows*

How to Tell the Wild Animals

If ever you should go by chance
    To jungles in the East;
And if there should to you advance
    A large and tawny beast,
If he roars at you as you're dyin'
You'll know it is the Asian Lion.

Or if some time when roaming round,
    A noble beast greets you,
With black stripes on a yellow ground,
    Just notice if he eats you.
This simple rule may help you learn
The Bengal Tiger to discern.

If strolling forth, a beast you view,
    Whose hide with spots is peppered,
As soon as he has lept on you,
    You'll know it is the Leopard.
'Twill do no good to roar with pain,
He'll only lep and lep again.

—*Carolyn Wells*

The Hummingbird Explains

"How flattering," muttered the hummingbird,
"That you find my fluttering pretty."

"And I'm glad you can see that I'm just being me
When I'm acting so flighty and flitty."

"But think not that I'm dumb when I constantly hum—
Though the true reason why is absurd."

"I can sing very well if I want. You can tell!
It's just that I don't know the words!"

—Randall Simms

Camels' Marching Song
From "Parade Song of the Camp Animals"

Can't! Don't! Shan't! Won't!
Pass it along the line!
Somebody's pack has slid from his back,
'Wish it were only mine!
Somebody's load has tipped in the road—
Cheer for a halt and a row!

Urr! Yarrh! Grr! Arrh!
Somebody's catching it now!

—*Rudyard Kipling*

The Puffin

Upon this cake of ice is perched
The paddle-footed Puffin;
To find his double we have searched,
But have discovered—Nuffin!

—*Robert Williams Wood*

The Personable Porcupine

Now a young porcupine
Makes a passable pet,
Though he sneezes and snorts
If his prickles get wet.

So bathe him with caution
And dry him with care,
Shampoo well his whiskers
And massage his hair.

He's tender and loving,
A fair dinkum friend
Whose sweet disposition
I well recommend.

There's no need to sing him
Asleep of a night,
Just tell him a story
And tuck him in tight.

He'll scare away lap-dogs
Cockroaches and rats,
And frighten the life
out of unwary cats.

He likes pickled parsnips,
Baked bananas and bread;
But one word of warning—
Keep him out of your bed!

—*Wilbur G. Howcroft*

47

A Puppy

A puppy whose hair was so flowing
There really was no means of knowing
Which end was his head,
Once stopped me and said,
"Please, sir, am I coming or going?"

—Oliver Herford

Rats!
from " The Pied Piper of Hamlin "

Rats!
They fought the dogs and killed the cats . . .
And ate the cheeses out of the vats . . .
Split open the kegs of salted sprats,
Made nests inside men's Sunday hats
And even spoiled the women's chats,
By drowning their speaking
    With shrieking and squeaking
In fifty different sharps and flats.

—Robert Browning

As I Went to Bonner

As I went to Bonner,
  I met a pig
  Without a wig,
Upon my word and honor.

—*Mother Goose*

Utter Nonsense

Somebody Being a Nobody

Somebody being a nobody,
Thinking to look like a somebody,
Said that he thought me a nobody:
Good little somebody-nobody,
Had you not known me a somebody,
Would you have called me a nobody?

—*Alfred, Lord Tennyson*

From "You Are Old, Father William"

"You are old, Father William," the young man said,
"And your hair has become very white;
And yet you incessantly stand on your head—
Do you think, at your age, it is right?"

"In my youth," Father William replied to his son,
"I feared it might injure the brain;
But, now that I'm perfectly sure I have none,
Why, I do it again and again!"

—Lewis Carroll

The Roof

The roof it has a lazy time,
  A-lying in the sun;

The walls, they have to hold him up;
  They do not have much fun!

—*Gelett Burgess*

A Peanut

A peanut sat on a railroad track,
  His heart was all a-flutter;
The five-fifteen came rushing by—
  Toot! toot! peanut butter!

—*American Folk Rhyme*

The Fate of the Flimflam

A flimflam flopped from a fillamaloo,
    Where the pollywog pinkled so pale,
And pipkin piped a petulant "pooh"
    To the garrulous gawp of the gale.
"Oh, woe to the swap of the sweeping swipe
    That booms on the bobbling bay!"
Snickered the snark to the snoozing snipe
    That lurked where the lamprey lay.

The gluglug glinked in the glimmering gloam,
    Where the buzbuz bumbled his bee—
When the flimflam flitted, all flecked with foam,
    From the sozzling and succulent sea.
"Oh, swither the swipe, with its sweltering sweep!"
    She swore as she swayed in a swoon,
And a doleful dank dumped over the deep,
    To the lay of the limpid loon!

—*Eugene Field*

Topsy-Turvy World

If the butterfly courted the bee,
    And the owl and the porcupine;
If churches were built in the sea,
    And three times one was nine;
If the pony rode his master,
    If the buttercups ate the cows,
If the cats had the dire disaster
    To be worried, sir, by the mouse;
If mamma, sir, sold the baby
    To a gypsy for half a crown;
If a gentleman, sir, was a lady,—
    The world would be Upside-down!
If any or all of these wonders
    Should ever come about,
I should not consider them blunders,
    For I should be Inside-out.

—William Brighty Rands

$3 \times 1 = 9$?

THE END!